Where Does Breakfast Come From?

Contents

D1498564

Rigby

Breakfast

This family is having breakfast.

What are they eating?

milk

eggs

bread

cornflakes

orange juice

Where does this food come from?

Where does milk come from?

1 Milk comes from cows.

2 Farmers milk the cows.

3 The milk goes to a factory.

4 The milk is put into containers.

Where do eggs come from?

1 Eggs come from chickens.
Chickens lay eggs.

2 The eggs go to a factory.

3 The eggs are
put into cartons.

Where does bread come from?

Bread is made from wheat.

Farmers grow wheat.

The wheat is cut.

2 The wheat goes to a mill.
It is turned into flour.

3 The flour is made into bread.

Where do cornflakes come from?

1 Cornflakes come from corn. Farmers grow corn.

2 The corn is cut.

3 The corn goes to a factory.

4 The corn is turned into cornflakes.

Where does orange juice come from?

1 Oranges grow on trees.

2 Some oranges go to supermarkets.

2 Some oranges go to factories.
They are squeezed to make juice.

3 The oranges
are squeezed
by hand.

3 The orange
juice is put into
containers.

Breakfast Chart

Milk

Eggs

Bread

Cornflakes

Orange juice

or

a
b
c
d
e
f
g
h
i
j
k
l
m
n
o
p
q
r
s
t
u
v
w
x
y
z

Index

 chickens 6

 corn 10

 cows 4

 oranges 12

 wheat 8